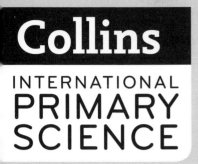

Collins

INTERNATIONAL PRIMARY SCIENCE

T0318015

Workbook 2

William Collins' dream of knowledge for all began with the publication of his first book in 1819. A self-educated mill worker, he not only enriched millions of lives, but also founded a flourishing publishing house. Today, staying true to this spirit, Collins books are packed with inspiration, innovation and practical expertise. They place you at the centre of a world of possibility and give you exactly what you need to explore it.

Collins. Freedom to teach.

Published by Collins
An imprint of HarperCollins*Publishers* Ltd.
The News Building
1 London Bridge Street
London
SE1 9GF

HarperCollins*Publishers*
Macken House,
39/40 Mayor Street Upper,
Dublin 1,
D01 C9W8,
Ireland

> **Browse the complete Collins catalogue at www.collins.co.uk**

© HarperCollins*Publishers* Limited 2021

10 9 8 7

ISBN: 978-0-00-836894-4

Second edition

Contributing authors: Karen Morrison, Tracey Baxter, Sunetra Berry, Pat Dower, Helen Harden, Pauline Hannigan, Anita Loughrey, Emily Miller, Jonathan Miller, Anne Pilling, Pete Robinson.

British Library Cataloguing in Publication Data
A Catalogue record for this publication is available from the British Library.

Commissioning editor: Joanna Ramsay
Product manager: Letitia Luff
Development editor: Karen Williams
Project manager: 2Hoots Publishing Services Ltd
Proofreader: Caroline Low
Cover designer: Gordon MacGilp
Cover illustrator: Ann Paganuzzi/John Batten (Beehive Illustration)
Image researcher: Emily Hooton
Illustrators: Beehive Illustration (John Batten, Moreno Chiacchiera, Phil Garner, Kevin Hopgood, Tamara Joubert, Andrew Pagram, Simon Rumble, Jorge Santillan, Matt Ward)
Internal design and typesetting: Ken Vail Graphic Design Ltd
Production controller: Lyndsey Rogers
Printed and bound by: Replika Press Pvt. Ltd, India

With thanks to the following teachers and schools for reviewing materials in development: Preeti Roychoudhury, Sharmila Majumdar and Sujata Ahuja, Calcutta International School; Hawar International School; Melissa Brobst, International School Budapest; Rafaella Alexandrou, Diana Dajani, Sophia Ashiotou and Adrienne Enotiadou, Pascal Primary School Lefkosia; Niki Tzorzis, Pascal Primary School Lemesos; Vijayalakshmi Chillarige, Manthan International School; Taman Rama Intercultural School.

Acknowledgements
The publishers wish to thank the following for permission to reproduce photographs.
Every effort has been made to trace copyright holders and to obtain their permission for the use of copyright materials. The publishers will gladly receive any information enabling them to rectify any error or omission at the first opportunity.

p1 Felix Lipov/Shutterstock, p6t EcoPrint/Shutterstock, p6tc Jacqui Martin/Shutterstock, p6bc Armin Rose/ Shutterstock, p6bc Alexey Kamenskiy/Shutterstock, p31a grynold/Shutterstock, p31b Werner Muenzker/ Shutterstock, p31c Aleksandr Bryliaev/shutterstock, p31d Dragan Milovanovic/Shutterstock, p31e Crepesoles/ Shutterstock, p31f Ron Dale/Shutterstock, p39 Alexey Kamenskiy/Shutterstock, p41 3DMI/Shutterstock, p55tl cosma/Shutterstock.com, p55tc Rudchenko Liliia/Shutterstock, p55tr SueC/Shutterstock, p55cl holbox/Shutterstock, p55c irin-k/Shutterstock, p55r Pavel Semenov/Shutterstock, p55bl Igor Kovalchuk/ Shutterstock, p55bc Pincarel/Shutterstock, p55br Dmitriy Eremenkov/Shutterstock.

Registered Cambridge International Schools benefit from high-quality programmes, assessments and a wide range of support so that teachers can effectively deliver Cambridge Primary.
Visit www.cambridgeinternational.org/primary to find out more.

Contents

Topic 5 Light and electricity

Topic 6 The Earth's crust

Student's Book p **2**

1.1 Asking questions

Complete the questions

Look at the photograph and complete the questions about it.

What would happen if	Why is/are	How does/do

When	What does/do	Where

Student's Book p **4**

1.2 What is an environment?

A home environment

This is Mandla's environment.

1 Colour all the plants and animals you can see in Mandla's environment.

2 Name three natural things in Mandla's environment.

_____

_____

_____

3 Think about how Mandla's environment is similar or different to your home environment.

   a Write two ways Mandla's environment is similar.

   _____

   b Write two ways Mandla's environment is different.

_____

Student's Book p **6**

1.3 Compare natural environments

Compare natural environments

1 Match the type of environment with its picture and the conditions found there.

2 Now colour the matching boxes the same colour.

rainforest

rocky, high, cold, windy

mountains

hot, dry, barren

grasslands

flat, grassy

desert

humid, hot, wet, fertile

Student's Book p **8**

1.4 Plants in different habitats

Where do plants grow?

1 Where would you expect to find these plants?
Talk about how you could find out the answer to this question.
Write the names of the plants in the correct columns in the table.

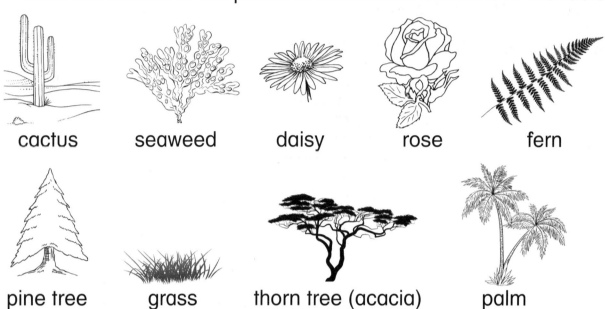

cactus   seaweed   daisy   rose   fern

pine tree   grass   thorn tree (acacia)   palm

Hot and wet	Hot and dry	Cold with snow	Sea or ocean

2 Add at least one plant of your own to each of these environments.

Student's Book p **8**

1.4 Plants in different habitats

Different habitats

Your teacher will help you to find two different habitats around your school or local area. Draw and label some of the plants and animals that live in each habitat.

Habitat 1:_____

Habitat 2:_____

Animals in different habitats

Draw lines to match each animal on the left to a suitable habitat.

giraffe

polar bear

hare

whale

eagle

fish

antelope

goat

crab

grassland

ocean

polar region

mountains

Student's Book p **10**

1.5 Animals in different habitats

Which words?

1 Choose words from the box that mean the same as:

a An area that has not been changed by people:

_____

b An area that has buildings like schools and homes in it:

_____

c The place an animal or plant lives in:

_____

d Something that protects an animal from bad weather or danger:

_____

2 Use red to circle the words that name three things all animals need in their habitats.

3 Use blue to circle the words that describe the conditions in different environments.

> cold   dry   food   habitat   hot   shelter   water   wet
> built environment   natural environment

Student's Book p **12**

1.6 Exploring local environments

What we found

1 At the bottom of the graph, write the plants you found.

2 Colour in the blocks in each column to show how many plants of each type you found. Use a different colour for each column.

10						
9						
8						
7						
6						
5						
4						
3						
2						
1						

Student's Book p **14**
1.7 Investigate a local environment

Local plant fact file

Choose one plant that grows well in your local environment.

My plant is a _____

Draw or stick a picture of your plant in the box opposite.

1 Where does your plant grow?

_____

_____

_____

_____

2 Describe the soil in which your plant grows.

   a What does the soil look like?

_____

   b What does the soil feel like?

_____

   c Is the soil wet or dry? _____

3 Why do you think your plant grows so well in your local environment? Give two reasons.

_____

_____

_____

Student's Book p 14

1.7 Investigate a local environment

Investigate your own environment

1 Where will you do your investigation?

_____

2 What small animals do you expect to find there?

_____

3 What will you do to make sure you are safe?

_____

_____

4 What do you need to take with you?

_____

_____

5 Make a drawing of the environment you are investigating.

continued ➡

6 Complete this table to show what you found.

Type of small animal	Where it was found	How many there were

7 Where did you find the most small animals in this environment?

_____

8 Why do you think most small animals were found there?

_____

_____

9 How are you going to present your findings to the class?

_____

_____

_____

10 Was the environment suitable for small animals?

Yes ☐   No ☐

Why? _____

Student's Book p **18**

2.1 Humans and other animals

Similar and different

1 Tick the blocks that are true for each animal.

	human	cat	bird	fish	snake	tortoise
head						
body						
arms/ legs						
wings						
fins						
hair						
feathers						
scales						
shell						

continued ➡

2 Use the information in the table to help you complete these sentences.

a All the animals have a _____ and a

_____.

b Only the _____ has wings.

c Only the _____ has fins.

d Only the _____ has a shell.

e The animals that have arms or legs are the

_____, _____,

_____ and

_____.

f The human and the cat have _____

that covers their bodies.

g The _____ and the

_____ have scales on their bodies.

h The _____ has feathers.

Student's Book p **20**

2.2 Animals and their offspring

Animal families

1 Draw a line to match each baby animal to its family.

2 Which baby animals change a lot when they grow into adults?

_____

3 Which baby animals do not change a lot when they grow into adults?

_____

_____

Student's Book p **22**
2.3 Do we look like our parents?

Shared features

Fill in this table for your family or the pictures your teacher has given you.

Features	Parent 1	Parent 2	Child
eye colour			
hair colour			
skin colour			
curly or straight hair			
tall or short			
freckles			
dimples			

1 Which features are shared with parent 1?

_____

_____

2 Which features are shared with parent 2?

_____

_____

Student's Book p **22**

2.3 Do we look like our parents?

What will the baby look like?

1 Colour in the pictures of these two creatures.

2 Draw a picture to show what you think their baby would look like.

Colour code your food

1 Colour the meat, dairy and eggs red.

2 Colour the potatoes and things made from potato yellow.

3 Colour all the fruit and vegetables green.

4 Colour the foods you should eat less of brown.

Student's Book p **24**

2.4 Keeping healthy

The kitchen cupboard

Draw the foods from the list in this cupboard.
Try to put each food on the correct shelf.

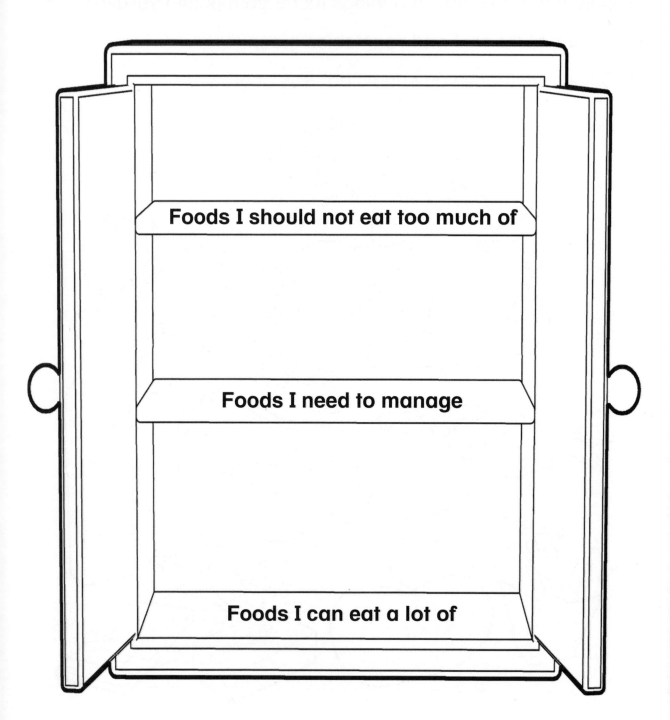

Foods I should not eat too much of

Foods I need to manage

Foods I can eat a lot of

Student's Book p **26**

2.5 Diet and exercise
are important

A healthy meal

Create a healthy menu for your class for a day.

Student's Book p **26**

2.5 Diet and exercise are important

My favourite form of exercise

1 Draw a picture of yourself doing the form of exercise you like.

2 Now write a paragraph to explain why you think this form of exercise is good for you.

_____

_____

_____

_____

Student's Book p **28**
2.6 Signs of illness

Who is sick?

Look at the pictures and read the sentences.
Write the correct child's name under each picture.

Amy has a high fever.

Cindy is very tired.

Liam has a terrible headache.

Mia can't stop coughing.

Oliver has a sore stomach.

Rosa has a blocked nose.

Tim has a sore throat.

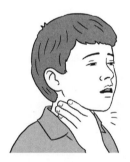  

_____ _____ _____

   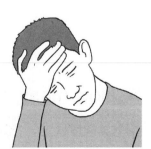

_____ _____ _____ _____

Student's Book p **30**
2.7 Human teeth

Different kinds of teeth

1 Write the names of the different kinds of teeth in the boxes.

2 Colour all the **incisors** blue.

3 Colour all the **canines** green.

4 Colour all the **premolars** yellow.

5 Colour all the **molars** red.

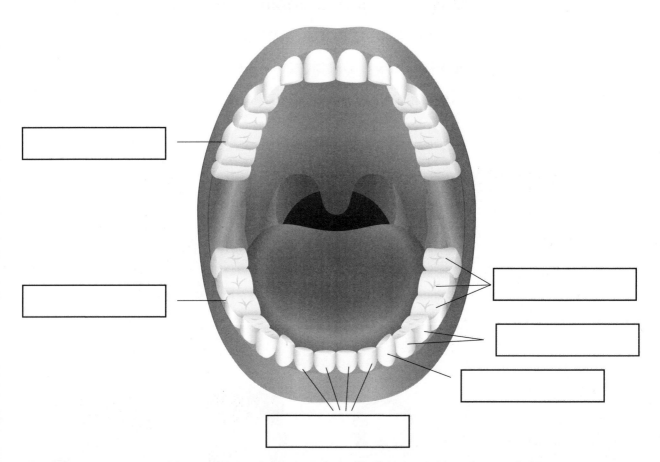

6 How many of each kind are there? Complete the table.

incisors	canines	premolars	molars	total number of teeth

What our teeth do

1 Colour the boxes in column **A** different colours.

2 Colour the boxes in columns **B** and **C** to show which ones match with the boxes in column **A**.

A	B	C
incisors	big wide teeth	They help crush and grind your food while you chew.
canines	flat teeth	They help cut your food.
premolars and molars		They all help to break your food into smaller pieces so that you can swallow it easily.
all teeth	pointed teeth	They help tear your food.

Student's Book p **32**

2.8 Dentists and science

Science and our teeth

1 Draw a red circle around the things that we use at home to look after our teeth.

2 Draw a green circle around the things that a dentist uses to look after your teeth.

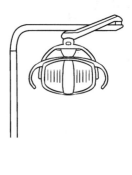

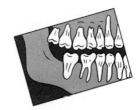

Student's Book p **34**

Looking back Topic 2

What did you learn?

Choose words from the box to complete the sentences.

> flexible   six   feathers   fever   manage   wings
> offspring   headache   life cycle   protein

1 Birds have _____ that cover their skin.

2 Birds use their _____ to fly.

3 The changes an animal goes through during its life is called its

_____.

4 We should _____ the amount of sugary foods

we eat.

5 Exercise makes you strong and _____.

6 Two symptoms of illness are a _____ and a

_____.

7 Most children start getting permanent teeth when they are

_____ years old.

8 _____ are the babies of adult animals.

Student's Book p **36**
3.1 Measuring

Measuring

1 Predict which object is wider: the door or the window?

_____

2 What objects will you use to measure:

the door? _____

the window? _____

3 Record your measurements.

	Measurement
Door	
Window	

4 Use your measurements to decide which is wider: the door or the window.

_____

5 Is your answer in (4) the same as what you predicted in (1)?

_____

Where does it come from?

1 Colour each word a different colour.

rocks plants animals

2 Colour the objects to match the words and show whether they come from rocks, plants or animals.

pencil

silk scarf

cotton shirt

paper cup

leather sandals

paper

table

fur boots

feather duster

diamond ring

clay pot

knitted clothes

bricks

wooden toy

wall

straw hat

27

Student's Book p **38**
3.2 Natural materials

Materials from plants and animals

Complete this mind map to show what materials we get from plants.

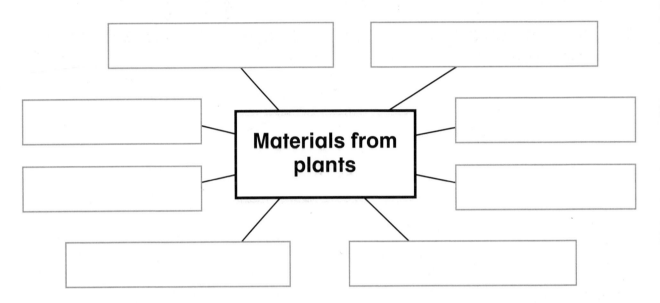

Complete this mind map to show what materials we get from animals.

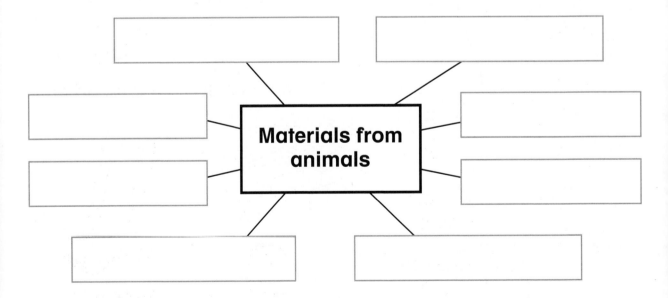

Student's Book p **40**

3.3 Manufactured materials

Manufactured objects in my home

Find six objects in your home that were made by people or in a factory. Stick or draw a picture of each object in the table.

Complete the table.

Manufactured objects in my home	
Name of object _____ Picture of object Materials used to make it: _____	Name of object _____ Picture of object Materials used to make it: _____
Name of object _____ Picture of object Materials used to make it: _____	Name of object _____ Picture of object Materials used to make it: _____
Name of object _____ Picture of object Materials used to make it: _____	Name of object _____ Picture of object Materials used to make it: _____

Student's Book p **40**

3.3 Manufactured
materials

Plastic search

1 Find and colour all the objects in this picture
that could be made from plastic.

2 How many objects did you find? _____

Student's Book p **42**
3.4 Properties of materials

What are its properties?

Describe the properties of the materials in each object.

Object	Properties
glass block	
straw bale	
pot	
rubber gloves	
sponge	
drinking glass	

Student's Book p **42**

3.4 Properties of materials

Comparing two metals

Investigate the properties of two metal objects.

Talk to your partner about what you could do to find out the answers to the questions. What investigations could you do?

Record your findings in the table.

Property	Paperclip	Metal spoon
Is the metal hard?		
Is the metal heavy?		
Is the metal smooth?		
Can you bend the metal?		
Can you break the metal?		
Is the metal shiny?		
Can you see through the metal?		
What colour is the metal?		

Student's Book p **44**

3.5 Hard or soft?

Rub test

Rub the object over the material being tested. Make sure you rub for the same amount of time and with the same pressure every time.

Rubbing object	Material being tested by rubbing	Is the material scratched during rubbing?	Which material is harder?

Student's Book p **44**
3.5 Hard or soft?

Dent test

1 Drop the object from the same height onto another material.

- If the object being dropped puts a dent into the material it falls on, the material being hit is softer.

- If there is no dent, then the material being hit is harder.

2 Record the results of your dent test here.

Object being dropped	Material being tested by being hit	Is there a dent?	Which material is harder?

Student's Book p **46**
3.6 Strength

How strong?

1 How much did you put in the container before the material broke?

Material being tested	Made or natural?	How many weights did you put on before it broke?

2 Rank the materials in order from the strongest to the weakest.

_____

_____

Student's Book p **48**

3.7 Flexibility

Fit for the job

1 Write the important property for each object and the material you would choose.

2 Give reasons for your choices.

Object	Property needed	Material chosen	Reasons
floor			
hammer			
table			
cushion			
bag			

Student's Book p **48**
3.7 Flexibility

How flexible?

1 Predict how flexible each material will be, on a scale of 1 to 4 (1 is the least flexible and 4 is the most flexible). Write your predictions in the table below.

Material	My prediction (1, 2, 3 or 4)	My findings (1, 2, 3 or 4)

2 Now test the objects.

3 Did the results match your predictions? _____

4 Explain why. _____

_____

_____

_____

_____

Student's Book p **48**

3.7 Flexibility

Inflatable life jackets

1 Fill in the gaps to describe how an inflatable life jacket works. Use the words in the box.

> air   float   balloon   squashes

An inflatable life jacket is like a _____. It fills with

_____ when the cord is pulled quickly. This means

that the person will _____ safely in the water.

2 Draw a picture of an inflatable life jacket and label it.

Student's Book p **50**

3.8 Uses of materials

Car parts

Look at the picture of the car.

1 Write the important property for each part of the car and the material you would choose.

2 Give reasons for your choices.

Car part	Property	Material chosen	Reasons

Student's Book p **52**
3.9 Changing materials

Change the materials

Describe how you can change three materials into different materials.

Material	What can you do to change the material?	Draw a picture to show the new material
jelly powder		
egg		
wooden popsicle stick		

Student's Book p **54**

3.10 Sports equipment

What is it made of?

Talk to your partner about how you could find out what a tennis racket is made from.

Label the tennis racket to show what materials modern tennis rackets are made from.

Student's Book p 56
Looking back Topic 3

Find the words

1 Colour the pairs of words that are opposites in the same colour.

2 Find all the words in the wordsearch block.

> flexible   hard   heat   natural   properties   purpose   rigid
> rough   smooth   soft

c	x	i	t	d	p	s	o	v	e
p	n	a	t	u	r	a	l	e	f
u	s	n	s	m	o	o	t	h	l
r	i	g	i	d	p	d	o	o	e
p	o	p	e	z	e	y	p	t	x
o	r	j	h	a	r	d	s	e	i
s	p	m	u	k	t	a	c	h	b
e	h	u	b	g	i	e	w	e	l
r	o	u	g	h	e	m	p	a	e
p	r	w	a	c	s	o	f	t	e

Draw a diagram

1 Draw a diagram that shows how your model works.
Include arrows and the words *push* and *pull* in your diagram.

2 Write some sentences to explain your diagram.

_____

_____

_____

_____

Student's Book p **60**

4.2 Forces and movement

Stopping a ball

1 How can you stop a moving ball?
Record your ideas in the table below.

2 Use a tick to show which ideas will work for a ball that is thrown and which will work for a ball that is rolled.

Ways to stop a ball	Will work for a ball that is thrown	Will work for a ball that is rolled

3 Colour in the blocks to show which of your ideas worked.

Student's Book p **60**

4.2 Forces and movement

How forces stop movement

Create a diagram to show how to move and stop a ball.
Use labels to show how the forces work.

Which force?

Student's Book p **62**
4.3 Changing the shape of an object

Label the pictures using force words from the box.

push   pull   stretch   squash   squeeze

Topic **4** Forces

Student's Book p **62**
4.3 Changing the shape
of an object

Working with clay

1 Model some shapes with your clay.
Then draw the clay before and after.

Before	After

2 Use the force words in the box to help you describe what you did.

push together   pull apart   stretch   squeeze

_____

_____

_____

_____

Student's Book p **62**

4.3 Changing the shape
of an object

Working with metal

1 Research how forces can be used to shape metal.

2 Complete the table. Write what is being done to the metal
in the first column and what kind of force is used in the
second column.

Action	Force

3 Complete the sentences.

Forces are useful in metal work because _____

_____

Before they were made by machines, cars were made by _____

Investigating cars (1)

You are going to investigate which toy car moves the fastest.

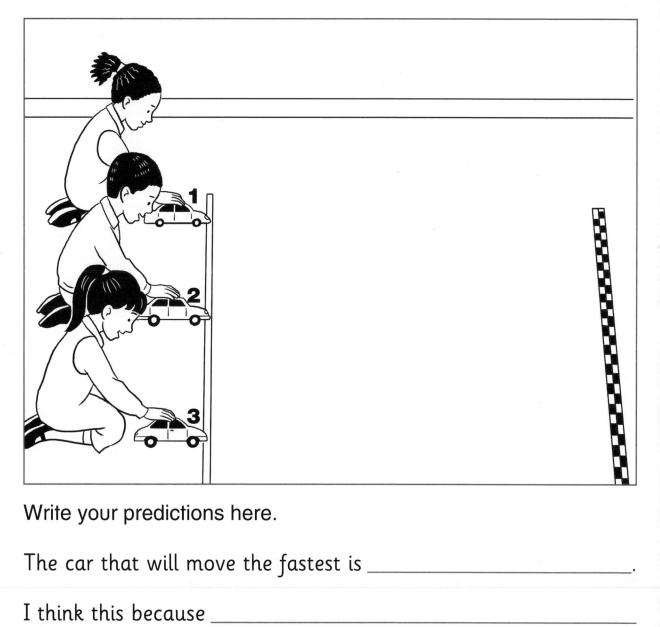

Write your predictions here.

The car that will move the fastest is _____ .

I think this because _____

_____

_____ .

Student's Book p **64**

4.4 Speeding up and slowing down

Investigating cars (2)

Draw or write your plan here.

Carry out your plan and record your results here.

Draw the position of each car after it was pushed.

continued

Measure how far each car travelled.

	Distance travelled
Car 1 – small push	
Car 2 – medium push	
Car 3 – big push	

Compare your results with your predictions here.

Which car won the race? _____

Which car was in second place? _____

Which car was in third place? _____

Which car moved the fastest? _____

Explain your results.

The winning car moved the fastest because _____

_____

_____

_____.

The more force we use, the _____ the car goes.

The less force we use, the _____ the car goes.

Student's Book p 66
4.5 Changing direction

Investigating rolling balls (1)

You are going to investigate what happens when you roll two balls towards each other.

Write your predictions here.

When the balls bump into each other _____

_____

_____ .

I think this because _____

_____ .

Draw or write your plan here.
Show what the two different balls look like.

Investigating rolling balls (2)

Carry out your plan and record your results here.

Draw the positions of the balls after they bump into each other.

Compare your results with your predictions here.

When the balls bumped into each other _____

_____

_____.

The balls changed direction because _____

_____.

Look back at your prediction. Were you correct?

Yes ☐   No ☐   Not sure ☐

Student's Book p **68**

Looking back Topic 4

Using force words

1 Use the words in the box to label the pictures.

bend   dent   faster   pull   push   slower   squeeze

_____   _____

_____   _____   _____

2 Can you write these words? Use the words in the box to help you.

a A word that means the same as **speed up**: _____

b A word that means the same as **slow down**: _____

c A word that means the opposite of **pull**: _____

Identify the light sources

1 Which of these things are sources of light?
Tick (✔) the light sources.

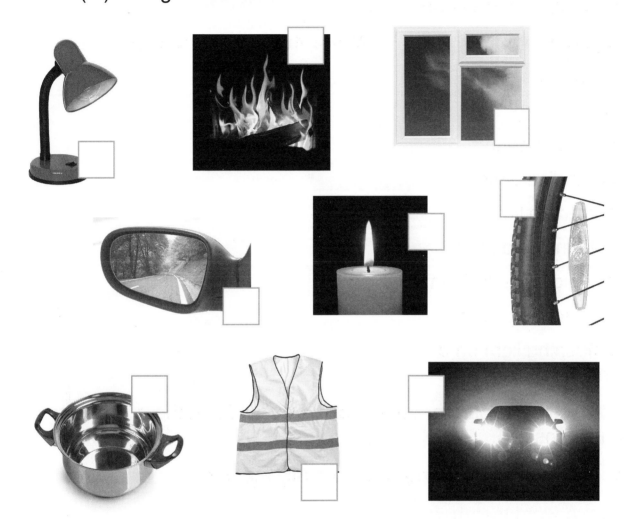

2 Use a red crayon to mark all the sources of light in this home.

Student's Book p **70**
5.1 Sources of light

Useful lights

Lights help us to see when it is dark, but they also have other uses.

1 Complete this chart.

Type of light	What the light is used for
traffic light	
street lamp	
car headlamp	
car indicator light	
car brake light	
light inside a fridge	
red indicator light on a TV	
a lit-up shop sign	
a flashing light on a mobile phone	

Talk with your partner about how you could find the answers to questions 2–4.

2 What does a flashing light normally mean?

_____

3 What do the red, yellow and green lights on a set of traffic lights mean?

_____

_____

4 Why do some lights stay on all the time?

Student's Book p **72**
5.2 Light and dark

What's in the box?

Look through the hole in the box.

Which things can you see clearly in the dark? Tick (✔) the correct column. Then choose three different objects to put in the box.

Inside the box there is a ...	I can see it clearly	I cannot see it clearly
pencil		
toy car		
flashlight (switched on)		
flashlight (switched off)		
mobile phone (screen on)		
mobile phone (screen off)		
small mirror		

57

Student's Book p **74**

5.3 Lighting in our homes

Light sources and lamps

1 Survey your home or school to find out which light sources there are. Write how many you find.

ceiling lights ☐   desk or table lights ☐

on/off display lights ☐   electronic screens ☐

flashlights ☐   other light sources ☐

2 Find out what sort of lamps are used in your home or school. Record your results in the table.

Type of lamp	Tally	Total
Fluorescent tube		
Long-life lamp (compact fluorescent)		
Filament lamp		
Halogen lamp		
LED		

Light sources

1 Use the words in the box to label the pictures.

2 Tick the light sources that use electricity.

paraffin lamp	long-life lamp	oil lamp fire
filament lamp	LED candle	paraffin lamp

☐

☐

☐

_____

_____

_____

☐

☐

☐

☐

_____

_____

_____

_____

Student's Book p **76**

5.4 Where is the Sun?

Where is the Sun?

1 Draw a picture of the area around your school.

2 Make observations of the Sun during the school day. Draw where the Sun is in the sky:

a in the morning when school starts

b at mid-morning break

c at lunchtime

d at home time.

Student's Book p **76**

5.4 Where is the Sun?

Sun questions

1 Why do you think 12 o'clock in the afternoon is called midday?

_____

2 The Sun rises in the east and sets in the west. Write where you think east and west are on your drawing.

3 Fill in the labels for **sunrise**, **midday** and **sunset** on this diagram.

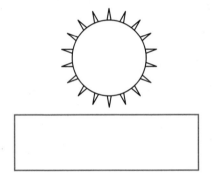

Student's Book p **78**
5.5 Using electricity

Electricity at school

Investigate your school environment by completing the table.

	Tally	Total
Electrical sockets in our classroom		
Things in our classroom that use electricity		
Electrical sockets in the passage outside our classroom		
Electrical sockets in the student's bathroom		
Electrical items that are not safe or not being used safely		

Student's Book p **80**
5.6 What is a circuit?

Circuit components

1 Complete this table.

Component	Name

2 Look at the drawings. Tick (✔) the ones that show a circuit.
Put a cross (✗) next to the ones that do not show a circuit.

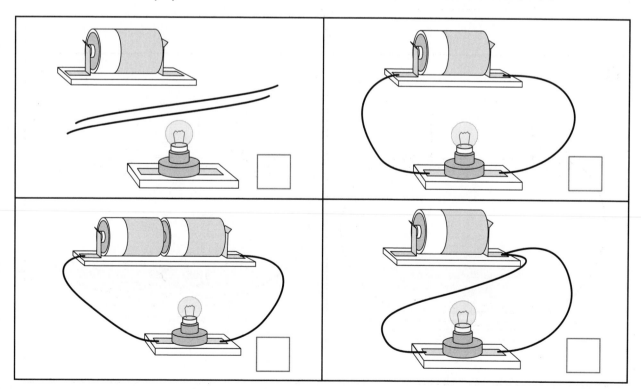

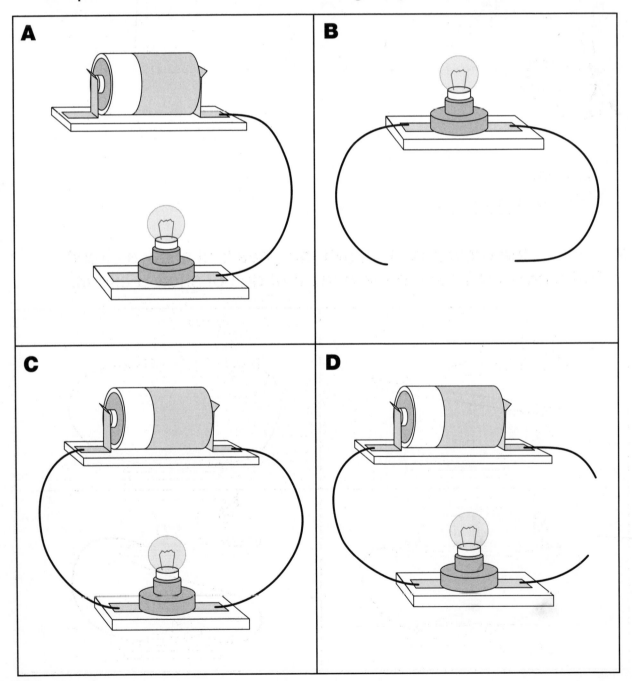

Student's Book p **80**

5.6 What is a circuit?

Missing components

1 Look at the four circuits below. Predict whether the lamp will light up in each circuit.

2 For any circuit that will not light up, draw in the missing component so that the circuit will light up.

A

B

C

D

Student's Book p **82**

5.7 Building circuits

Building circuits

1 Draw the circuit you built.

> A circuit with two lamps:

2 Draw and label three ways of connecting components so that the lamp lights up.

> Method 1:

> Method 2:

> Method 3:

Student's Book p 82

5.7 Building circuits

Sort out the instructions

Here is a set of instructions for building a circuit with two cells and two lamps.

Step 1: Collect all the components that you need.

Step 2: Connect the two cells together using a piece of wire.

Step 3: Connect a wire from the positive (+) side of the front cell to the first lamp.

Step 4: Connect the first lamp to the second lamp using a piece of wire.

Step 5: Connect a wire from the second lamp to the negative (–) side of the back cell.

These pictures have been mixed up. Number them from 1 to 5 to show the correct order for building the circuit.

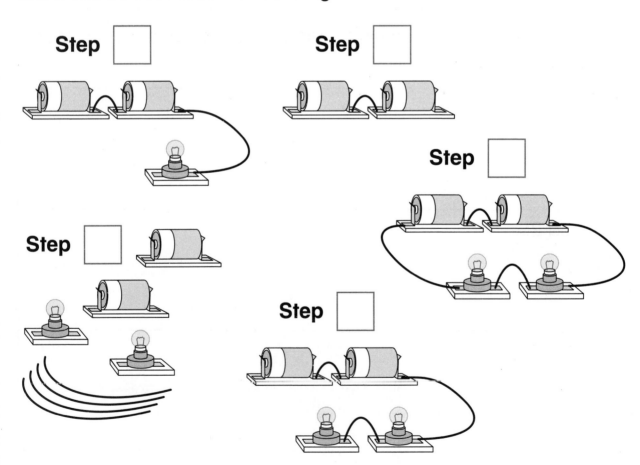

Step ☐

Step ☐

Step ☐

Step ☐

Step ☐

Student's Book p **84**
Looking back Topic 5

Using science words

1 Match the words in column A with their meanings in column B.
Colour each pair the same colour.

A	B
light source	a place that makes electricity
sunlight	the path that electricity follows
Earth	when it starts to get light
darkness	an object that gives out light
power station	parts of a circuit
sunrise	a circuit in which all the components are properly joined
sunset	the planet we live on
electrical circuit	light that comes from the Sun
closed circuit	when it starts to get dark
components	when there is no light

2 Choose two of the terms from A and use each one in a sentence.

_____

_____

Student's Book p **86**

6.1 Using sources

About mining

Stick the sentences about mining into the correct column of the table.

Advantages	Disadvantages

Student's Book p **88**
6.2 Different types of rocks

Looking at rocks

You will use a magnifying glass and observe three different rocks. Record your findings in the table.

	Rock 1	Rock 2	Rock 3
Name of rock			
Drawing or picture of rock			
Colour			
What does it feel like?			
Are there any crystals?			
Is it made from layers or tiny bits joined up?			
Is it shiny or dull?			

Student's Book p **88**

6.2 Different types of rocks

Testing the hardness of rocks

Plan a fair test to find out how hard different rocks are.

What equipment will you need?

_____

What will you measure/observe to collect your evidence?

_____

What will you do to make it a fair test?

_____

What is your procedure?

First we will _____ .

Then we will _____ .

After that we will _____ .

What did you find out?

_____

Put your rock samples in order from hardest to softest.

_____

If you did this test again, what would you change?

_____

Why?

_____

Rock search

Find some items made from rocks or stones.

Complete the table.

Item	Type of rock used	Why I think this rock was chosen to make this item

Student's Book p **92**

6.4 Mining the Earth

Draw a diagram

This is a diagram of _____ mine.

Student's Book p **92**
6.4 Mining the Earth

Comparing mines

1 Complete the table by putting a tick in the correct column.

	Open-pit mines	Underground mines	Mines in riverbeds
On the Earth's surface			
Deep in the Earth's crust			
Deep hole			
Has tunnels			
Minerals are dug out			
Stone is dug out			

2 Name the types of mines in the pictures.

a   **b**   **c**

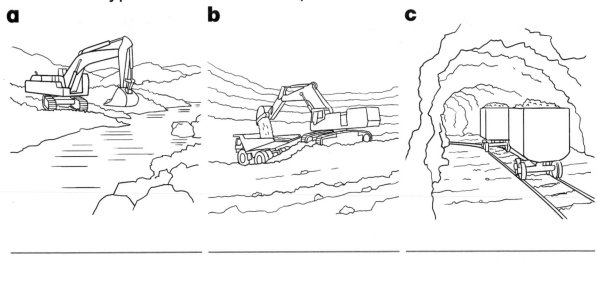

_____   _____   _____

_____   _____   _____

Student's Book p **94**

6.5 Mining in Madagascar

Before, during, after

Draw pictures to show how the environment changed.

Before mining

During mining

After the miners left

After planting

What did you read about?

Answer the questions about mining in Madagascar.

1 What was the environment like before mining started?

_____

2 What are the miners looking for?

_____

3 Why do they mine?

_____

4 Do they get sapphires out of the ground or out of rivers?

_____

5 Does mining make the miners rich?

_____

6 What happens when there are no more sapphires?

_____

7 What is the environment like when the miners leave?

_____

8 Underline the things that people are trying to do differently:

find more gold / help the miners earn a better living /

regrow the forests by planting new trees / buy better equipment

Student's Book p **94**
6.5 Mining in Madagascar

Information for better choices

When you have information about something, you can make better choices to keep yourself and your environment safe.

Work with a partner. Discuss and write down how artisanal miners can use information about the issues below to keep themselves and the environment safe.

Information about:

Where to mine

_____

_____

The best way to extract minerals

_____

_____

How to control soil erosion

_____

_____

How to prevent water pollution

_____

_____

Why healthy ecosystems are important

_____

_____

Think about what you learned

Complete these sentences by finding the correct ending in the box and writing it in the space under each sentence.

Endings:

… can help find solutions to the negative effects of mining

… will lead to safer mining practices.

… quarry for money for their families.

… need to be rehabilitated.

… provides jobs for many people

1 Small-scale artisanal mining …

_____

2 Children from poor families …

_____

3 Scientific investigations …

_____

4 Abandoned pits and mining tunnels …

_____

5 Information on the importance of ecosystems …

_____

Student's Book p **96**
Looking back Topic 6

Match words and their meaning

1 For each description below, find one word in the box that means the same.

| properties minerals extract riverbed mine pit environment |

a valuable chemicals that are found in the ground

_____

b take out or remove _____

c qualities that materials have that make them useful

_____

d the ground over which a river flows _____

e a large hole in the ground _____

f a hole or tunnel dug in the ground so that people can extract

materials _____

g the place around you _____

2 Write a sentence with each of these words in it:

mining: _____

dig: _____

Language focus

Match the word in the box to its definition, then complete the puzzle.

> quarry   properties   unique   irregular   extract
> abandoned   marble   minerals   artisanal   machinery

Across

1 valuable chemicals that are found in the ground

3 unusual and special

5 not having a fixed shape

8 a group of large machines

10 take out or remove

Down

2 done in a traditional way

4 dig for stone or rock

6 left behind

7 qualities that an object has which makes it useful

9 beautiful stone used to carve statues and monuments

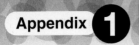
Electrical symbols

Cell	
Battery of cells	
Wire	
Lamp	
Junction of conductors	
Open Switch	
Closed Switch	
Buzzer	